MW00911006

Dropping In On...

MEXICO

Lewis K. Parker

A Geography Series

ROURKE BOOK COMPANY, INC.
VERO BEACH, FLORIDA 32964

A Blackbirch Graphics book.

Printed in the United States of America.

Library of Congress Cataloging-in-Publication Data

Parker, Lewis K.
    Dropping in on Mexico / Lewis K. Parker.
        p.   cm.
    Includes index.
    ISBN 1-55916-001-2
    1. Mexico—Description and travel—Juvenile literature. [1. Mexico—Description and travel.] I. Title.
        F1208.5.P37   1994
        917.204'855—dc20   93-42777
                                    CIP
                                    AC

Mexico
■■■■■■■■■■

Official Name: **United Mexican States**

Area: **761,600 square miles**

Population: **92,381,000**

Capital: **Mexico City**

(Federal District)

Largest City: **Mexico City**

Highest Elevation:

Volcán Citlaltépetl

(18,700 feet)

Official Language: **Spanish**

Major Religion: **Roman Catholic**

Money: **Peso**

Form of Government:

Federal Republic

TABLE OF CONTENTS

Our Blue Ball—The Earth

The Earth can be divided into two hemispheres. The word hemisphere means "half a ball"—in this case, the ball is the Earth.

The equator is an imaginary line that runs around the middle of the Earth. It separates the Northern Hemisphere from the Southern Hemisphere. North America—where Canada, the United States, and Mexico are located—is in the Northern Hemisphere.

The Northern Hemisphere

When the North Pole is tilted toward the sun, the sun's most powerful rays strike the northern half of the Earth and less sunshine hits the Southern Hemisphere. That is when people in the Northern Hemisphere enjoy summer. When

the North Pole is tilted away from the sun, and the Southern Hemisphere receives the most sunshine, the seasons reverse. Then winter comes to the Northern Hemisphere. Seasons in the Northern Hemisphere and the Southern Hemisphere are always opposite.

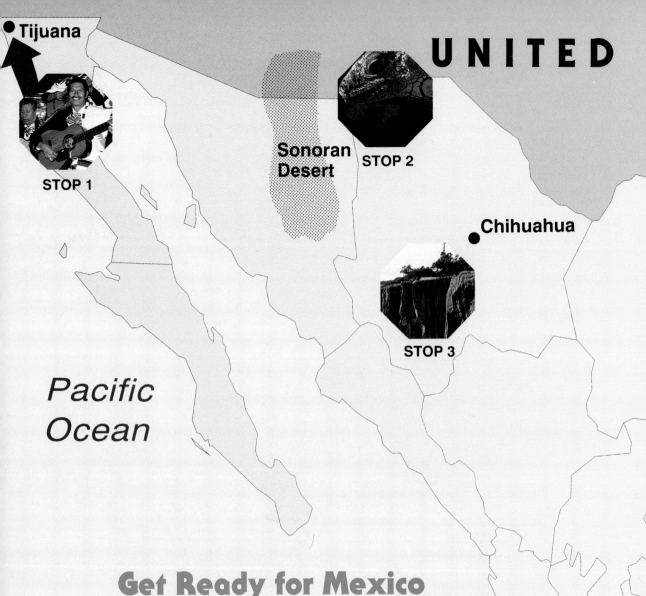

● Tijuana

STOP 1

Sonoran Desert

STOP 2

● **Chihuahua**

STOP 3

Pacific Ocean

Get Ready for Mexico

Hop into your hot-air balloon. Let's take a trip! You are about to drop in on the third-largest country in North America. Mexico is about one fourth the size of the United States. More than 90 million people live here.

N
W   E
S

STOP 5

Mexico

⭐ National Capital

0   Miles   300

Gulf of Mexico

STOP 7

STOP 4

Chichen Itza

THE
YUCATAN
PENINSULA

STOP 6

Rainforests

**Mexico
City** ⭐
Distrito
Federal

BELIZE

Acapulco
●

GUATEMALA

HONDURA

Golfo de Tehuantepec

Left: Tourists shop and browse in an outdoor market in Tijuana. Top: A mariachi band plays for a crowd. Bottom: A young woman displays colorful flowers in a Mexican store.

Stop 1: Tijuana

Our first stop is Tijuana. It is a large city just across the *frontera*. The *frontera* is the border between Mexico and the United States. About 2 million people live in Tijuana. Every day, thousands of tourists visit this city. Most of these tourists travel from the United States.

People often visit Tijuana to eat in its many restaurants. Others prefer buying *tortillas* and *tacos* from carts that sellers push through the crowded streets. People can relax on the white sand of Tijuana's beaches or go deep-sea fishing in the Pacific Ocean. Many also go to see the bullfights on Sunday afternoons, or to shop in Tijuana's many outdoor markets. While they shop, people can listen to the music of *mariachi* bands playing guitars, trumpets, and violins. The city of Tijuana also has many business offices and a number of interesting museums.

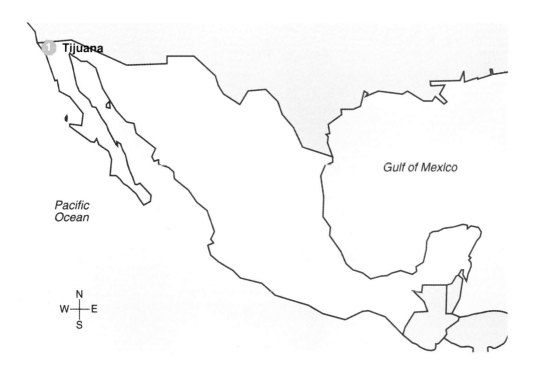

*Let's travel **southeast** to visit a rugged desert.*

Stop 2: The Sonoran Desert

The Sonoran Desert stretches from Arizona south to Mexico. This is a very dry area that only receives about 3 inches of rain a year. Sand dunes, salt flats, and boulders cover the land.

Stubby plants called desert scrub cover much of the desert. Many kinds of cactuses also grow here. Some of these prickly plants, such as the

Iguanas, like this one, enjoy the hot, dry climate of Mexican deserts.

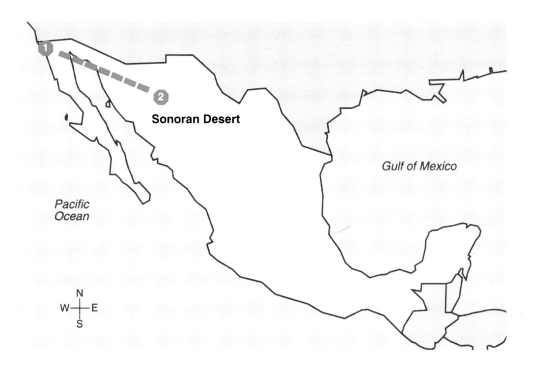

saguaro cactus, can grow 50 feet tall! One plant, the boojum, can live for a very long time—some are 600 years old!

Among the desert's trees and bushes live many animals, such as iguanas, Gila monsters, and horned lizards. During the cool of the night, diamondback rattlesnakes slither across the sand in search of their prey. Elf owls perched on the arms of tall cactuses watch cougars prowl through the darkness.

*Now it is time to head for our next location.We'll float on winds that carry us **southeast** to Chihuahua.*

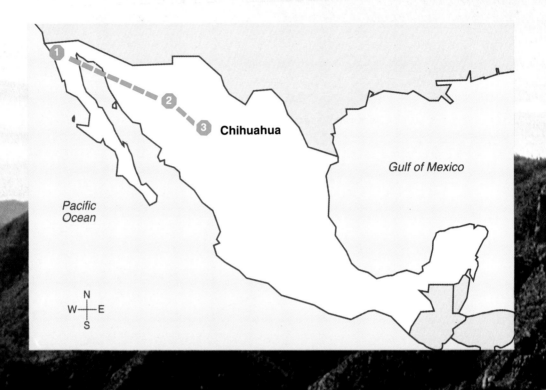

Stop 3: Chihuahua

The Sierra Madres are mountains that run like a backbone down through Mexico. Most of this area is desert country. There are several large cities here, such as Chihuahua.

Chihuahua means "dry and sandy place" in 2 Indian languages. Chihuahua is where you may start a train ride through Barranca del Cobre, known as Copper Canyon.

The Copper Canyon train twists its way thousands of feet up the mountains and spins around steep cliffs and canyon walls.

Copper Canyon's breathtaking mountains and cliffs are often explored by visitors.

Tarahumara Indians live in caves tucked away like pockets in the walls of Copper Canyon. The Tarahumaras live in much the same way as their ancestors did thousands of years ago.

Our next stop is Mexico City. To get there, we'll travel **southeast** down the central plateau of Mexico.

Stop 4: Mexico City

Mexico City is the capital of Mexico. It sits on a dry lake bed in a high valley. It is surrounded on 3 sides by mountains. It is not easy to see this beautiful city clearly from the air. On most days, thick smog hides the city, which covers almost 600 square miles. The smog is caused by thousands of buses, cars, and factories. It is no wonder Mexico City has the world's worst pollution problem—it has the second-largest population in the world. About 20 million people live here.

A good place to start our visit in Mexico City is at the Zócalo (plaza) in the downtown area. Mexico's National Palace is in the Zócalo. The president of Mexico has his offices in the palace. The Metropolitan Cathedral is also in the Zócalo. It is the largest cathedral in Latin America.

The giant Metropolitan Cathedral in downtown Mexico City is over 400 years old.

Gulf of Mexico

Pacific
Ocean

Mexico City

1

2

3

4

Just east of the Zócalo is La Merced, the largest food market in the world. Farmers from all over Mexico bring food to sell here. There are papayas, mangoes, fried turtles, steamed chicken intestines, steamed crayfish, lichee nuts, *charales* (corn husks stuffed with fish), and 2 blocks of all kinds of chiles. The market also has 5 blocks of *dulces* (sweets) with each stand selling many kinds.

Before leaving the area, you may want to visit Teotihuacan. This ancient Aztec city is about 30 miles from Mexico City. Thousands of years ago, it was the center of Aztec culture and contained as many as 200,000 people. The center of the city has a series of plazas and a center street that leads to pyramids. These pyramids were built by people who lived in the valley long before the Aztecs arrived. The Pyramid of the Sun was built 1,850 years ago. It is the world's third-largest pyramid, is as tall as a 20-story skyscraper, and has 248 steeply rising steps.

Opposite: At night, the buildings and streets of Mexico City sparkle.

LET'S TAKE TIME OUT

Beans, rice, and corn are the main foods eaten in Mexico. Sometimes they can be very spicy!

The Foods of Mexico

In Mexico, the main meal of the day is usually eaten between 2 and 4 P.M. It is called the *comida*. A lot of food is eaten at this time. The most common dishes include *botanas* (snacks), *sopa aguada* (thin soup), *sopa seca* (dry pasta soup), meat or chicken, beans, and dessert. *Agua fresca* is a very popular drink. This is water flavored with lemon or orange seeds.

Each area of Mexico has its own special foods. Cooks in Mexico City may serve dead or live maguey worms in some dishes. The worms are covered with a hot sauce, tucked into tacos, and are very crunchy!

Corn is used in many Mexican dishes. The ears and husks are used for *tamales*. The corn silk is made into tea. The dried kernels are crushed to make *masa* (tortilla dough).

*Next we'll travel **south** to the beautiful city of Acapulco. There, we can take a break from our travels and relax on the beautiful white sands of the city's many beaches.*

Pacific
Ocean

Gulf of Mexico

Acapulco

N
W—E
S

Stop 5: Acapulco

Before we land in Acapulco, look over the side of the balloon basket. You'll see the unusual shape of Acapulco. It forms a semi-circle around Acapulco Bay.

Thousands of people visit Acapulco every year because the city has a humid tropical climate. Even in January, the temperature stays about 80 degrees Fahrenheit. People also come because of the beautiful beaches covered with white sand.

Before we leave Acapulco, let's visit the La Quebrada cliffs. These cliffs are located just outside the city. They are famous for the divers who plunge about 120 feet straight down into the water.

*Now it's time to pull our ropes and set sail again. This time, we're heading **east** into the heart of Mexico's rainforest.*

Opposite: An Acapulco cliff diver flies through the air toward the water. Above: The sandy, semi-circular white beaches of Acapulco Bay invite many visitors to sun and swim each year.

Stop 6: Mexico's Rainforests

Mexico is not all dry desert or coastal resort cities—it is also a land of tropical rainforests. The southern end of the Yucatan Peninsula and the surrounding area is North America's largest rainforest. The thick trees of this forest are famous for *chicle*—a substance used to make chewing gum. Thousands of other green plants also thrive in this environment.

The hot, humid rainforest is filled with all kinds of wildlife. Brightly striped butterflies larger

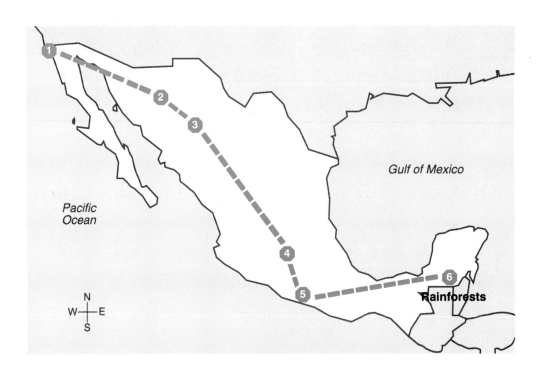

Opposite: In the Rancho de Cielo rainforest, a waterfall fills a pool below.

than your hand fly through the air and monkeys chatter and swing from tree to tree. Every so often you might see a jaguar slinking through the shadows. The rainforest is also the habitat for wild boar, giant spiders, and thousands of species of lizards and snakes.

*For our last stop we'll travel **northeast**. There, we'll camp on the Yucatan Peninsula and visit some ancient ruins.*

Stop 7: The Yucatan Peninsula

Some of the famous attractions of the Yucatan are the ancient Mayan ruins in Chichen Itza. Many tourists visit Chichen Itza each year. The site is filled with temples that are actually pyramids.

The most impressive pyramid here is El Castillo. The passageway is only open a few hours each day so you may want to visit it first. Two huge serpents are carved at the base of the structure. The pyramid was built so that on both the first day of spring and the first day of fall every year the shadow of the setting sun slowly moves up the staircase leading to the top. The pyramid has 4 staircases with 91 steps each. When the number of steps is added to the top platform, the total is 365, which is the number of days in a year. The serpent heads point straight to a natural well where human bones and jewelry have been found. This is the Well of Sacrifice. It is 115 feet deep and 197 feet wide. Ancient Mayans thought that the deep well was the home of the rain gods.

Opposite: The Mayan ruin, El Castillo, is located in Chichen Itza. To see the view from the top, you must climb 91 steps.

Pacific
Ocean

Gulf of Mexico

Yucatan
Peninsula

N
W — E
S

The Indians of Mexico

About 50 separate Indian groups live in Mexico. They are different in many ways, but they also share many similar customs.

Huichols. The Huichols live in mountains along the western area of Mexico. They plant corn, beans, and squash for food.

Coras. The Coras live near the Huichols. There are only a few Coras living in Mexico. They raise corn and a few other crops.

Totonacs. There are about 200,000 Totonacs in Mexico. They live in the tropical highlands of the Yucatan Peninsula. They use wild plants for medicines.

Seris. There are only about 500 Seris. They live along the Gulf of California and weave and sell beautiful baskets.

Lacandones. The Lacandones, who live far back in the rainforest jungle, worship the sun.

Tarahumaras. This group lives in the canyons and mountains of northern Mexico. They are known as great runners. Many run long distances—as far as 100 miles—without stopping.

Tzotzils and Tzeltals. These Indians live in the Mexican highlands. The Tzotzils dwell on the lower slopes of the mountains, while the Tzeltals live a bit higher up.

Now it's time to set sail for home. When you return, you can think back on the wonderful adventure you had in Mexico.

There are many different Indian groups living in Mexico. Here, a Mayan girl holds her sister.

Glossary

corridos Street ballads that are played by musicians.

frontera The border between Mexico and the United States.

habitat Surroundings or environment in which an animal or plant lives.

mariachi Street musicians who play guitars, trumpets, and violins.

Mayans Indian people who developed a great civilization thousands of years ago in Mexico and Central America.

plateau A raised, flat area of land that rises slightly above the surrounding land.

ruins The remains of something destroyed or decayed.

taco A beef, pork, or chicken mixture wrapped up in a tortilla.

tamale Steamed corn dough filled with meat, chile, or vegetables.

tortilla A flat cake made of cornmeal or wheat flour.

zócalo The center of a town, usually a plaza where the most important buildings are located.

Further Reading

Fisher, Leonard E. *Pyramid of the Sun—Pyramid of the Moon*. New York: Macmillan, 1988.

Flint, David. *Mexico*. Madison, NJ: Raintree Steck-Vaughn, 1993.

Gomez, P. *Food in Mexico*. Vero Beach, FL: Rourke, 1992.

Hicks, Peter. *The Aztecs*. New York: Thomson Learning, 1993.

Moran, Tom. *A Family in Mexico*. Minneapolis, MN: Lerner, 1987.

Sherrow, Victoria. *The Maya Indians*. New York: Chelsea House, 1993.

Silverthorne, Elizabeth. *Fiesta: Mexico's Greatest Celebrations*. Brookfield, CT: The Millbrook Press, 1992.

Index

Acknowledgments and Photo Credits
Cover: ©Carl Frank/Photo Researchers, Inc.; pp. 4, 6: National Aeronautics and
Space Administration; p. 10: ©Bernard P. Wolff/Photo Researchers, Inc. (left); pp.
10 (top and bottom), 14, 16, 18, 20, 22, 23, 27: ©Mexican Government Tourism
Office; p. 12: ©Kram Leopold/Gamma Liaison; p. 25: ©Emil Barsak/Gamma
Liaison; p. 29: ©Mark Downey/Liaison International.
Maps by Blackbirch Graphics, Inc.